DAILY LIGHT ON THE URBAN COMMUNITY

30-Day Scriptural Devotion for Social Justice and Social Change

BY DR. M.W. COUCH

Advanced Praise

"And the King shall answer and say unto them, Verily I say unto you, Inasmuch as ye have done it unto one of the least of these my brethren, ye have done it unto me" – Matthew25:40. Brothers and sisters, we must be concerned about the social and economic prosperity in our community 365 days of the year. The apostle Paul said in Philippians 3, "This one thing I do." Start by finding an issue in your community where you can help your brothers and sisters grow socially or economically throughout the year. Take the time today to pray about whether you have been called to feed the hungry, clothe the naked, or visit those in jail.

Reverend Dr. R. Leon Sewell
Solid Rock Missionary Baptist Church
Jacksonville, Florida

Dr. Michael W. Couch has written a devotional to remind us that God is concerned about the right treatment of humans and that we are to be involved in that process. Jesus' inaugural message was about justice and reaching out to those who received injustice. Luke 4:18 (KJV) says, "The Spirit of the Lord is upon me, because he hath anointed me to preach the gospel to the poor; he hath sent me to heal the brokenhearted, to preach deliverance to the captives, and recovering of sight to the blind, to set at liberty them that are bruised." I encourage you to get your copy today, and like Jesus, help bring healing to a hurting world.

Reverend Dr. G. Cornelius Jones
Global Ministry
Kansas City, Missouri

Rev. Couch has prepared in this pamphlet a unique set of divine office reflections for both morning and evening, designed to align the believer's heart and mind with the heart and Spirit of God.

R. Todd Mangum,
Ph.D. Clemens Professor of Missional Theology
Missio Seminary

This is a great Bible study and interactive reading guide. It was hard for me to put it down once I picked it up. Dr. Michael Couch's book is very user friendly and concise, packed with encouraging scriptures with unique, edifying, and spirit building questions. As a personal friend, I know for a fact that the Scriptures he has selected and teaches are the exact same verses he used to edify himself and build his very successful ministry. If it is possible, I have become a renewed fan of Dr. Couch, and when I read, studied, and interacted with his book, I was very lifted and impressed. While studying with his book, I had actually gone beyond my normal Bible reading and was immediately taken to a higher spiritual level in God's Word. Daily Light On The Urban Community will easily become your number one Bible supplement.

Dr. Titus C. Wright
Chairman of TWrightMediaGroup.com

DAILY LIGHT
on the URBAN
COMMUNITY
30-Day Scriptural Devotion for
Social Justice and Social Change

MORNING AND EVENING
With Additional Readings
for Special Occasions
By Dr. M.W. COUCH

ISBN 978-1-7359185–0-1 (paperback)

ISBN: 978-1-7359185-1-8 (ebook)

Dedication

This book is dedicated to my family, who have prayed for me and pushed me to thrive, Jessie Bridges (R.I.P), Rose Brides, Tonya Couch, My'chal Couch, and Malachi Couch.

In addition, I dedicate this book to my pastor, the Reverend Dr. Robert P. Shine, Sr. and mentors who have poured into me the wisdom of social justice and civic engagement.

This book is dedicated to Reverend Leslie Wilson, Director of the African American Religious Affairs, The Women of VASHTI, African American Ministers Leadership Council, African American Ministers In Action, Micah Leadership Council, and VESSELS-VOTE.

Lastly, this book is dedicated to my seven brothers, Reverend Arlington Medley, Reverend Malcolm Medley, Reverend Harry Chaney, Laurence Richardson, Sean Hawkins, John Lindsay, and William Everett.

Acknowledgments

By the grace of God, I was able to finish this book. I thank Dr. Darryl D. Sims for his mental sharpness and keen intelligence for being the wind in the sail of this book that finally came to the port of print. In addition, I owe so much to New York Theological Seminary (Micah Cohort) for their commitment to help formulate the proverbial out-of-the-box thinking that pushes seminaries to talk back without being apologetic. Also, I would like to thank my father for showing me how to fight without throwing a physical blow to the faces of the enemies of justice.

The completion of this project rests upon the shoulders of my wife, who believes in the work of civic engagement. I would be remiss not to thank my oldest son for the exceptional encouragement. Lastly, I want to express a sincere thank you to my youngest son, Malachi Couch, for his conscience courage to empower me to push past procrastination to finish this devotional. Love you, Prophet-Father.

Contents

Introduction

In all of our lives, we must seek to do the ultimate will of God. Since accepting Jesus as my Lord and Savior, I have always had an interest in fairness and justice for the people within the urban community. One of my favorite scriptures to live by is Amos 5:24, which says, "But let justice roll down like waters, and righteousness like an ever-flowing stream."

The theme of justice, *mishpat*, surfaces over and over again in the Old Testament, dominating the Bible as one of its most major themes. The term *mishpat* is related to the idea of "righteousness" (tsedaqah), as it is used in parallel. For example, of Abraham, God says, "Behold, your servant has found favor in your sight, and you have shown me great kindness in saving my life. But I cannot escape to the hills, lest the disaster overtake me and I die" (Genesis 19:19).

The LORD tells His people to live justly and rightly. Abraham was called to "charge his children and his household after him to… righteousness and justice." This is "the way of the Lord." To live in Yahweh's divine directive is to live as a person who evokes and teaches justice.

Near the beginning of Jesus' ministry, he enters a synagogue in Nazareth and reads from the prophet Isaiah. He concludes by saying, "Today this scripture has been fulfilled in your hearing" (Luke 4:21 NRSV). This is what Jesus said he fulfilled, "The Spirit of the Lord is upon me, because he has anointed me to bring good news to the poor. He has sent me to proclaim release to the captives and recovery of sight to the blind, to let the oppressed go free, to proclaim the year of the Lord's favor" (Luke 4:18-19 NRSV).

Meditate on those words. Jesus says he came "to bring good news to the poor...proclaim release to the captives...restore sight to the blind...to help the oppressed go free." If that's not a cry of justice, I don't know what is. Jesus came with the sheer intent of providing justice for the least of them as well as providing a way for salvation for everyone.

The Greek words used in Luke 4:18 for "bring good news" is *euangelizō*, which is the verbal form of the word usually translated as "gospel" (*euangelion*). One could translate this as Jesus saying, "because he [the Lord] has anointed me to bring the gospel to the poor."

Jesus defines his *gospel* as having a social component. It means the impoverished being lifted up; the "captive" to society's wrongful norms being released; the physically oppressed finding freedom. Social justice in the urban community points to Jesus' gospel, which is all about mortal justice and eternal salvation.

Jesus constantly taught his disciples the importance of prayer and justice. The Bible reports Jesus teaching his disciples a parable, "And he told them a parable to the effect that they ought always to pray and not lose heart. He said, "In a certain city there was a judge who neither feared God nor respected man. And there was a widow in that city who kept coming to him and saying, 'Give me justice against my adversary.' For a while he refused, but afterward he said to himself, 'Though I neither fear

God nor respect man, yet because this widow keeps bothering me, I will give her justice, so that she will not beat me down by her continual coming" (Luke 18:1-5).

Written with this in mind, my prayer is that this devotional book will elicit action to not just pray about social justice needs within our communities but encourage you to get involved. Who better to demand justice for all throughout the urban community than you, the faithful spiritual soldier of Jesus Christ? Who better to stand for those who feel as though they have no power? Who better to speak for those who feel they have no voice?

The devotional is designed to help you jumpstart the day with a call to action within your community. It is designed to help you focus on others as you seek to do God's will within your community. Also, it provides a space for you to record your activity from the day. It closes with a prayer focus topic for the evening and the next day.

It is clear that God's salient characteristic is love. Throughout scripture, we see the importance of loving our neighbors, but most importantly, loving God. Jesus taught that if a person makes the declaration that he/she truly loves him, then that person must keep his commandments. One of his commandments was for all believers to love one another as they love themselves and love God above all other things and people. I believe that there's a direct correlation between our love for Christ and our sacrifice for others. If one believes what Jesus declared, which is "we shall do greater things," then I'm sure seeking justice for the least of them is definitely included on the list.

Each day begins with Micah 6:8. This is a powerful reminder of God's expectation for us to be change agents here on earth. Then take a moment to meditate on the three provided scriptures that follow. Then allow God to reveal to you what issues and/or injustices you can address within your community. Write down 1-3 that you can refer to.

In the evening, read and reflect on the provided evening scripture. Then address the provided questions that will allow you to record how God used you to make a difference that day. End your day with a prayer that focuses on the daily suggested prayer emphasis.

Day 1

He has told you, O man, what is good; and what does the LORD require of you but to do justice, and to love kindness, and to walk humbly with your God? Micah 6:8

Morning

Job 12:22 He uncovers the deeps out of darkness and brings deep darkness to light.

Job 8:3 Does God pervert justice? Or does the Almighty pervert the right?

Matthew 23:23 Woe to you, scribes and Pharisees, hypocrites! For you tithe the mint and dill and cumin, and have neglected the weightier matters of the law: justice and mercy and faithfulness. These you ought to have done, without neglecting the others.

Ask God to show you a social justice issue in your community to do something about today.

1)
2)
3)

Evening

I have been young, and now am old; yet have I not seen the righteous forsaken, nor his seed begging bread. Psalm 37:25

Who did I help on today?
How did I help them?
How did I display God's love on today?

Prayer Emphasis: That the Holy Ghost will exalt His name in the community. (Exodus 34:5)

____
____
____
____
____
____
____
____

Day 2

He has told you, O man, what is good; and what does the LORD require of you but to do justice, and to love kindness, and to walk humbly with your God? Micah 6:8

Morning

Isaiah 1:16 Wash yourselves; make yourselves clean; remove the evil of your deeds from before my eyes; cease to do evil,

Jeremiah 22:3 Thus says the LORD: Do justice and righteousness, and deliver from the hand of the oppressor him who has been robbed. And do no wrong or violence to the resident alien, the fatherless, and the widow, nor shed innocent blood in this place.

Psalm 37:23-24 The steps of a man are established by the LORD, when he delights in his way; though he fall, he shall not be cast headlong, for the LORD upholds his hand.

Ask God to show you a social justice issue in your community to do something about today.

1)
2)
3)

Evening

Nevertheless, I am continually with you; you hold my right hand. You guide me with your counsel, and afterward you will receive me to glory. Psalm 73:23-24

Who did I help on today?
How did I help them?
How did I display God's love on today?

Prayer Emphasis: That the Holy Ghost will extend His Kingdom in this community. (Matthew 6:10)

____
____
____
____
____
____
____
____

Day 3

He has told you, O man, what is good; and what does the LORD require of you but to do justice, and to love kindness, and to walk humbly with your God? Micah 6:8

Morning

Proverbs 21:15 When justice is done, it is a joy to the righteous but terror to evildoers.

Amos 5:24 But let justice roll down like waters, and righteousness like an ever-flowing stream.

Romans 12:19 Beloved, never avenge yourselves, but leave it to the wrath of God, for it is written, "Vengeance is mine, I will repay, says the Lord."

Ask God to show you a social justice issue in your community to do something about today.

1)
2)
3)

Evening

The heavens declare his righteousness, for God himself is judge! Selah Psalm 50:6

Who did I help on today?
How did I help them?
How did I display God's love on today?

Prayer Emphasis: That the Holy Ghost will burden His people for justice in this community. (John 4:34)

____
____
____
____
____
____
____
____

Day 4

He has told you, O man, what is good; and what does the LORD require of you but to do justice, and to love kindness, and to walk humbly with your God? Micah 6:8

Morning

Isaiah 1:17 Learn to do good; seek justice, correct oppression; bring justice to the fatherless, plead the widow's cause.

Isaiah 30:18 Therefore the Lord waits to be gracious to you, and therefore he exalts himself to show mercy to you. For the Lord is a God of justice; blessed are all those who wait for him.

Isaiah 61:8 For I the Lord love justice; I hate robbery and wrong; I will faithfully give them their recompense, and I will make an everlasting covenant with them.

Ask God to show you a social justice issue in your community to do something about today.

1)
2)
3)

Evening

Therefore, since we are surrounded by so great a cloud of witnesses, let us also lay aside every weight, and sin which clings so closely, and let us run with endurance the race that is set before us, looking to Jesus, the founder and perfecter of our faith, who for the joy that was set before him endured the cross, despising the shame, and is seated at the right hand of the throne of God. Hebrews 12:1-2

Who did I help on today?
How did I help them?
How did I display God's love on today?

Prayer Emphasis: That the Holy Ghost will unite "Prayer Partners" who will stand together for justice for the community. (Luke 10:2)

____
____
____
____
____
____

Day 5

He has told you, O man, what is good; and what does the LORD require of you but to do justice, and to love kindness, and to walk humbly with your God? Micah 6:8

Morning

Psalm 106:3 Blessed are they who observe justice, who do righteousness at all times!

Proverbs 24:24-25 Whoever says to the wicked, "You are in the right," will be cursed by peoples, abhorred by nations, but those who rebuke the wicked will have delight, and a good blessing will come upon them.

Zechariah 7:9 "Thus says the LORD of hosts, Render true judgments, show kindness and mercy to one another,

Ask God to show you a social justice issue in your community to do something about today.

1)
2)
3)

Evening

Sing aloud to God our strength; shout for joy to the God of Jacob! Raise a song; sound the tambourine, the sweet lyre with the harp. Psalm 81:1

Who did I help on today?
How did I help them?
How did I display God's love on today?

Prayer Emphasis: That the Holy Ghost will reveal "persons of justice" in this community. (Acts 10 and 16)

____

____

____

____

____

____

____

____

Day 6

He has told you, O man, what is good; and what does the LORD require of you but to do justice, and to love kindness, and to walk humbly with your God? Micah 6:8

Morning

Leviticus 19:15 "You shall do no injustice in court. You shall not be partial to the poor or defer to the great, but in righteousness shall you judge your neighbor.

Ecclesiastes 3:17 I said in my heart, God will judge the righteous and the wicked, for there is a time for every matter and for every work.

Proverbs 28:5 Evil men do not understand justice, but those who seek the LORD understand it completely.

Ask God to show you a social justice issue in your community to do something about today.

1)
2)
3)

Evening

Have I not commanded you? Be strong and courageous. Do not be frightened, and do not be dismayed, for the LORD your God is with you wherever you go." Joshua 1:9

Who did I help on today?
How did I help them?
How did I display God's love on today?

Prayer Emphasis: That the Holy Ghost will give "wonders and signs" among the community that need justice. (James 5:17-18)

____
____
____
____
____
____
____
____

Day 7

He has told you, O man, what is good; and what does the LORD require of you but to do justice, and to love kindness, and to walk humbly with your God? Micah 6:8

Morning

Luke 6:37 "Judge not, and you will not be judged; condemn not, and you will not be condemned; forgive, and you will be forgiven;

Psalm 33:5 He loves righteousness and justice; the earth is full of the steadfast love of the LORD.

Romans 13:4 For he is God's servant for your good. But if you do wrong, be afraid, for he does not bear the sword in vain. For he is the servant of God, an avenger who carries out God's wrath on the wrongdoer.

Ask God to show you a social justice issue in your community to do something about today.

1)
2)
3)

Evening

Besides this you know the time, that the hour has come for you to wake from sleep. For salvation is nearer to us now than when we first believed. The night is far gone; the day is at hand. So then let us cast off the works of darkness and put on the armor of light. Let us walk properly as in the daytime, not in orgies and drunkenness, not in sexual immorality and sensuality, not in quarreling and jealousy. But put on the Lord Jesus Christ, and make no provision for the flesh, to gratify its desires. Romans 13:11-14

Who did I help on today?
How did I help them?
How did I display God's love on today?

Prayer Emphasis: That the Holy Ghost will empower children of God to stand up for justice. (Acts 4:29)

____

____

____

____

____

Day 8

He has told you, O man, what is good; and what does the LORD require of you but to do justice, and to love kindness, and to walk humbly with your God? Micah 6:8

Morning

Proverbs 21:3 To do righteousness and justice is more acceptable to the LORD than sacrifice.

Deuteronomy 16:20 Justice, and only justice, you shall follow, that you may live and inherit the land that the LORD your God is giving you.

Proverbs 25:26 Like a muddied spring or a polluted fountain is a righteous man who gives way before the wicked.

Ask God to show you a social justice issue in your community to do something about today.

1)
2)
3)

Evening

Consequently, he is able to save to the uttermost those who draw near to God through him, since he always lives to make intercession for them. Hebrews 7:25

Who did I help on today?
How did I help them?
How did I display God's love on today?

Prayer Emphasis: That the Holy Ghost will speak to those in authority in the community for justice. (Daniel 6:25-27)

Day 9

He has told you, O man, what is good; and what does the LORD require of you but to do justice, and to love kindness, and to walk humbly with your God? Micah 6:8

Morning

Deuteronomy 27:19 "'Cursed be anyone who perverts the justice due to the sojourner, the fatherless, and the widow.' And all the people shall say, 'Amen.'

Jeremiah 9:23-24 Thus says the LORD: "Let not the wise man boast in his wisdom, let not the mighty man boast in his might, let not the rich man boast in his riches, but let him who boasts boast in this, that he understands and knows me, that I am the LORD who practices steadfast love, justice, and righteousness in the earth. For in these things I delight, declares the LORD."

Matthew 7:12 "So whatever you wish that others would do to you, do also to them, for this is the Law and the Prophets.

Ask God to show you a social justice issue in your community to do something about today.

1)
2)
3)

Evening

Pray without ceasing, I Thessalonians 5:17

Who did I help on today?
How did I help them?
How did I display God's love on today?

Prayer Emphasis: That the Holy Ghost will bring peace and love to permeate this community. (Psalm 122:6-9)

____
____
____
____
____
____
____
____

Day 10

He has told you, O man, what is good; and what does the LORD require of you but to do justice, and to love kindness, and to walk humbly with your God? Micah 6:8

Morning

Jeremiah 22:3 Thus says the LORD: Do justice and righteousness, and deliver from the hand of the oppressor him who has been robbed. And do no wrong or violence to the resident alien, the fatherless, and the widow, nor shed innocent blood in this place.

Proverbs 31:8-9 Open your mouth for the mute, for the rights of all who are destitute. Open your mouth, judge righteously, defend the rights of the poor and needy.

Deuteronomy 10:18 He executes justice for the fatherless and the widow, and loves the sojourner, giving him food and clothing.

Ask God to show you a social justice issue in your community to do something about today.

1)
2)
3)

Evening

Open to me the gates of righteousness, that I may enter through them and give thanks to the LORD. Psalm 119:18

Who did I help on today?
How did I help them?
How did I display God's love on today?

Prayer Emphasis: That the Holy Ghost will bring together believers seeking God's glory in the community. (Acts 10:30-33)

____

____

____

____

____

____

____

____

Day 11

He has told you, O man, what is good; and what does the LORD require of you but to do justice, and to love kindness, and to walk humbly with your God? Micah 6:8

Morning

Isiah 42:1 Behold my servant, whom I uphold, my chosen, in whom my soul delights; I have put my Spirit upon him; he will bring forth justice to the nations.

Matthew 5:38-39 You have heard that it was said, 'An eye for an eye and a tooth for a tooth.' But I say to you, Do not resist the one who is evil. But if anyone slaps you on the right cheek, turn to him the other also.

Isaiah 56:1 Thus says the LORD: "Keep justice, and do righteousness, for soon my salvation will come, and my righteousness be revealed.

Ask God to show you a social justice issue in your community to do something about today.

1)
2)
3)

Evening

Therefore, my beloved, as you have always obeyed, so now, not only as in my presence but much more in my absence, work out your own salvation with fear and trembling, for it is God who works in you, both to will and to work for his good pleasure. Philippians 2:12-13

Who did I help on today?
How did I help them?
How did I display God's love on today?

Prayer Emphasis: For the grace of God to protect this community. (I Timothy 2:1-2)

Day 12

He has told you, O man, what is good; and what does the LORD require of you but to do justice, and to love kindness, and to walk humbly with your God? Micah 6:8

Morning

Psalm 58:11 Mankind will say, "Surely there is a reward for the righteous; surely there is a God who judges on earth."

Luke 11:42 "But woe to you Pharisees! For you tithe mint and rue and every herb, and neglect justice and the love of God. These you ought to have done, without neglecting the others.

Luke 4:18-19 "The Spirit of the Lord is upon me, because he has anointed me to proclaim good news to the poor. He has sent me to proclaim liberty to the captives and recovering of sight to the blind, to set at liberty those who are oppressed, to proclaim the year of the Lord's favor."

Ask God to show you a social justice issue in your community to do something about today.

1)
2)
3)

Evening

Do not be anxious about anything, but in everything by prayer and supplication with thanksgiving let your requests be made known to God. Philippians 4:6

Who did I help on today?
How did I help them?
How did I display God's love on today?

Prayer Emphasis: For discernment in recognizing God's hand and leadership in the community. (Philippians 1:9-10)

____

____

____

____

____

____

____

____

Day 13

He has told you, O man, what is good; and what does the LORD require of you but to do justice, and to love kindness, and to walk humbly with your God? Micah 6:8

Morning

Hosea 12:6 "So you, by the help of your God, return, hold fast to love and justice, and wait continually for your God."

Isaiah 56:1 Thus says the LORD: "Keep justice, and do righteousness, for soon my salvation will come, and my righteousness be revealed.

Psalm 101:1 I will sing of steadfast love and justice; to you, O LORD, I will make music.

Ask God to show you a social justice issue in your community to do something about today.

1)
2)
3)

Evening

Know therefore that the Lord thy God, he is God, the faithful God, which keepeth covenant and mercy with them that love him and keep his commandments to a thousand generations, Deuteronomy 7:9

Who did I help on today?
How did I help them?
How did I display God's love on today?

Prayer Emphasis: That the Holy Ghost will thrust "laborers of the gospel" in this community. (Matthew 9:38)

Day 14

He has told you, O man, what is good; and what does the LORD require of you but to do justice, and to love kindness, and to walk humbly with your God? Micah 6:8

Morning

Psalm 82:3 Give justice to the weak and the fatherless; maintain the right of the afflicted and the destitute.

Proverbs 29:7 A righteous man knows the rights of the poor; a wicked man does not understand such knowledge.

Isaiah 61:8-9 For I the Lord love justice; I hate robbery and wrong; I will faithfully give them their recompense, and I will make an everlasting covenant with them. Their offspring shall be known among the nations, and their descendants in the midst of the peoples; all who have shall acknowledge them, that they are an offspring the LORD has blessed.

Ask God to show you a social justice issue in your community to do something about today.

1)
2)
3)

Evening

If we endure, we will also reign with him; if we deny him, he also will deny us; II Timothy 2:12

Who did I help on today?
How did I help them?
How did I display God's love on today?

Prayer Emphasis: That those in positions of influence in and over this community may exalt Jesus Christ. (Psalm 67:3-4)

Day 15

He has told you, O man, what is good; and what does the LORD require of you but to do justice, and to love kindness, and to walk humbly with your God? Micah 6:8

Morning

Proverbs 31:9 Open your mouth, judge righteously, defend the rights of the poor and needy.

Psalm 140:12 I know that the LORD will maintain the cause of the afflicted, and will execute justice for the needy.

Deuteronomy 32:4 "The Rock, his work is perfect, for all his ways are justice. A God of faithfulness and without iniquity, just and upright is he.

Ask God to show you a social justice issue in your community to do something about today.

1)
2)
3)

Evening

Cast your burden on the LORD, and he will sustain you; he will never permit the righteous to be moved. Psalm 55:22

Who did I help on today?
How did I help them?
How did I display God's love on today?

Prayer Emphasis: That those faith leaders in the community live in holiness and godliness. (1 Thessalonians 1:9-10)

Day 16

He has told you, O man, what is good; and what does the LORD require of you but to do justice, and to love kindness, and to walk humbly with your God? Micah 6:8

Morning

James 1:27 Religion that is pure and undefiled before God the Father is this: to visit orphans and widows in their affliction, and to keep oneself unstained from the world.

Zechariah 7:9-10 "Thus says the LORD of hosts, Render true judgments, show kindness and mercy to one another, do not oppress the widow, the fatherless, the sojourner, or the poor, and let none of you devise evil against another in your heart."

Amos 5:15 Hate evil, and love good, and establish justice in the gate; it may be that the LORD, the God of hosts, will be gracious to the remnant of Joseph.

Ask God to show you a social justice issue in your community to do something about today.

1)
2)
3)

Evening

He saved us, not because of works done by us in righteousness, but according to his own mercy, by the washing of regeneration and renewal of the Holy Spirit, whom he poured out on us richly through Jesus Christ our Savior, Titus 3:5-6

Who did I help on today?
How did I help them?
How did I display God's love on today?

Prayer Emphasis: That the Holy Ghost will reveal specific areas and human needs needing divine intervention. (Mark 9:25-29)

Day 17

He has told you, O man, what is good; and what does the LORD require of you but to do justice, and to love kindness, and to walk humbly with your God? Micah 6:8

Morning

Ecclesiastes 5:8 If you see in a province the oppression of the poor and the violation of justice and righteousness, do not be amazed at the matter, for the high official is watched by a higher, and there are yet higher ones over them.

Psalm 89:14 Righteousness and justice are the foundation of your throne; steadfast love and faithfulness go before you.

Matthew 12:18 "Behold, my servant whom I have chosen, my beloved with whom my soul is well pleased. I will put my Spirit upon him, and he will proclaim justice to the Gentiles.

Ask God to show you a social justice issue in your community to do something about today.

1)
2)
3)

Evening

And we all, with unveiled face, beholding the glory of the Lord, are being transformed into the same image from one degree of glory to another. For this comes from the Lord who is the Spirit. II Corinthians 3:18

Who did I help on today?
How did I help them?
How did I display God's love on today?

Prayer Emphasis: That the Holy Ghost will reveal the felt needs of persons in the community. (Acts 17:22)

____
____
____
____
____
____
____
____

Day 18

He has told you, O man, what is good; and what does the LORD require of you but to do justice, and to love kindness, and to walk humbly with your God? Micah 6:8

Morning

Colossians 3:25 For the wrongdoer will be paid back for the wrong he has done, and there is no partiality.

Psalm 7:6 Arise, O LORD, in your anger; lift yourself up against the fury of my enemies; awake for me; you have appointed a judgment.

Isaiah 51:4-5 "Give attention to me, my people, and give ear to me, my nation; for a law will go out from me, and I will set my justice for a light to the peoples. My righteousness draws near, my salvation has gone out, and my arms will judge the peoples; the coastlands hope for me, and for my arm they wait.

Ask God to show you a social justice issue in your community to do something about today.

1)
2)
3)

Evening

Train up a child in the way he should go; even when he is old he will not depart from it. Proverbs 22:6

Who did I help on today?
How did I help them?
How did I display God's love on today?

Prayer Emphasis: That the Holy Ghost will provide for those who will be faith leaders to this community. (Romans 15:30-32)

Day 19

He has told you, O man, what is good; and what does the LORD require of you but to do justice, and to love kindness, and to walk humbly with your God? Micah 6:8

Morning

Isaiah 45:21 Declare and present your case; let them take counsel together! Who told this long ago? Who declared it of old? Was it not I, the LORD? And there is no other god besides me, a righteous God and a Savior; there is none besides me.

1 John 3:17-18 But if anyone has the world's goods and sees his brother in need, yet closes his heart against him, how does God's love abide in him? Little children, let us not love in word or talk but in deed and in truth.

James 4:1-2 What causes quarrels and what causes fights among you? Is it not this, that your passions are at war within you? You desire and do not have, so you murder. You covet and cannot obtain, so you fight and quarrel. You do not have, because you do not ask.

Ask God to show you a social justice issue in your community to do something about today.

1)
2)
3)

Evening

Trust in the LORD with all your heart, and do not lean on your own understanding. Proverbs 3:5

Who did I help on today?
How did I help them?
How did I display God's love on today?

Prayer Emphasis: That the Holy Ghost will enable faith leaders to love lost persons in the community as Jesus Christ loves them. (Matthew 19:19)

____

____

____

____

____

____

____

____

Day 20

He has told you, O man, what is good; and what does the LORD require of you but to do justice, and to love kindness, and to walk humbly with your God? Micah 6:8

Morning

Isaiah 61:1 The Spirit of the Lord GOD is upon me, because the LORD has anointed me to bring good news to the poor; he has sent me to bind up the brokenhearted, to proclaim liberty to the captives, and the opening of the prison to those who are bound;

Isaiah 5:23 Who acquit the guilty for a bribe, and deprive the innocent of his right!

Proverbs 18:5 It is not good to be partial to the wicked or to deprive the righteous of justice.

Ask God to show you a social justice issue in your community to do something about today.

1)
2)
3)

Evening

Blessed be the God and Father of our Lord Jesus Christ! According to his great mercy, he has caused us to be born again to a living hope through the resurrection of Jesus Christ from the dead, 1 Peter 1:3

Who did I help on today?
How did I help them?
How did I display God's love on today?

Prayer Emphasis: That the Holy Ghost will raise up faith leaders who are passionate about reaching this community. (Philippians 1:12-14)

____
____
____
____
____
____
____
____

Day 21

He has told you, O man, what is good; and what does the LORD require of you but to do justice, and to love kindness, and to walk humbly with your God? Micah 6:8

Morning

1 Peter 1:17 And if you call on him as Father who judges impartially according to each one's deeds, conduct yourselves with fear throughout the time of your exile,

Jeremiah 23:5 Behold, the days are coming, declares the LORD, when I will raise up for David a righteous Branch, and he shall reign as king and deal wisely, and shall execute justice and righteousness in the land.

Psalm 99:4 The King in his might loves justice. You have established equity; you have executed justice and righteousness in Jacob.

Ask God to show you a social justice issue in your community to do something about today.

1)
2)
3)

Evening

"Behold, the days are coming, declares the LORD, when I will raise up for David a righteous Branch, and he shall reign as king and deal wisely, and shall execute justice and righteousness in the land. Jeremiah 23:5

Who did I help on today?
How did I help them?
How did I display God's love on today?

Prayer Emphasis: That the Holy Ghost will show believers how to find favor in the eyes of the unchurched. (Acts 5:12-14)

____
____
____
____
____
____
____
____

Day 22

He has told you, O man, what is good; and what does the LORD require of you but to do justice, and to love kindness, and to walk humbly with your God? Micah 6:8

Morning

Romans 13:1 Let every person be subject to the governing authorities. For there is no authority except from God, and those that exist have been instituted by God.

Malachi 3:5 "Then I will draw near to you for judgment. I will be a swift witness against the sorcerers, against the adulterers, against those who swear falsely, against those who oppress the hired worker in his wages, the widow and the fatherless, against those who thrust aside the sojourner, and do not fear me, says the LORD of hosts.

Amos 5:7 O you who turn justice to wormwood and cast down righteousness to the earth!

Ask God to show you a social justice issue in your community to do something about today.

1)
2)
3)

Evening

If any of you lacks wisdom, let him ask God, who gives generously to all without reproach, and it will be given him. James 1:5

Who did I help on today?
How did I help them?
How did I display God's love on today?

Prayer Emphasis: That the Gospel will run and triumph in this community. (II Thessalonians 3:1)

____

____

____

____

____

____

____

____

Day 23

He has told you, O man, what is good; and what does the LORD require of you but to do justice, and to love kindness, and to walk humbly with your God? Micah 6:8

Morning

Isaiah 9:7 Of the increase of his government and of peace there will be no end, on the throne of David and over his kingdom, to establish it and to uphold it with justice and with righteousness from this time forth and forevermore. The zeal of the LORD of hosts will do this.

Psalm 119:126 It is time for the LORD to act, for your law has been broken.

2 Chronicles 9:8 Blessed be the LORD your God, who has delighted in you and set you on his throne as king for the LORD your God! Because your God loved Israel and would establish them forever, he has made you king over them, that you may execute justice and righteousness."

Ask God to show you a social justice issue in your community to do something about today.

1)
2)
3)

Evening

Masters, do the same to them, and stop your threatening, knowing that he who is both their Master and yours is in heaven, and that there is no partiality with him. Ephesians 6:9

Who did I help on today?
How did I help them?
What cause did I interject the presence of the Lord on today?

Prayer Emphasis: That the Holy Ghost will give visions of effectively reaching this community of gun violence to faith leaders. (Acts 18:9-10)

____

____

____

____

____

____

Day 24

He has told you, O man, what is good; and what does the LORD require of you but to do justice, and to love kindness, and to walk humbly with your God? Micah 6:8

Morning

2 Samuel 15:4 Then Absalom would say, "Oh that I were judge in the land! Then every man with a dispute or cause might come to me, and I would give him justice."

Revelation 19:11 Then I saw heaven opened, and behold, a white horse! The one sitting on it is called Faithful and True, and in righteousness he judges and makes war.

Luke 10:30 Jesus replied, "A man was going down from Jerusalem to Jericho, and he fell among robbers, who stripped him and beat him and departed, leaving him half dead.

Ask God to show you a social justice issue in your community to do something about today.

1)
2)
3)

Evening

"So you, by the help of your God, return, hold fast to love and justice, and wait continually for your God." Hosea 12:6

Who did I help on today?
How did I help them?
What cause did I interject the presence of the Lord on today?

Prayer Emphasis: That the Holy Ghost will save unbelievers in this community. (John 3:16)

Day 25

He has told you, O man, what is good; and what does the LORD require of you but to do justice, and to love kindness, and to walk humbly with your God? Micah 6:8

Morning

Isaiah 30:18-19 Therefore the LORD waits to be gracious to you, and therefore he exalts himself to show mercy to you. For he LORD is a God of justice; blessed are all those who wait for him. For a people shall dwell in Zion, in Jerusalem; you shall weep no more. He will surely be gracious to you at the sound of your cry. As soon as he hears it, he answers you.

Matthew 10:28 And do not fear those who kill the body but cannot kill the soul. Rather fear him who can destroy both soul and body in hell.

Malachi 4:1 "For behold, the day is coming, burning like an oven, when all the arrogant and all evildoers will be stubble. The day that is coming shall set them ablaze, says the LORD of hosts, so that it will leave them neither root nor branch.

Ask God to show you a social justice issue in your community to do something about today.

1)
2)
3)

Evening

"Thus says the LORD of hosts, Render true judgments, show kindness and mercy to one another, Zechariah 7:9

Who did I help on today?
How did I help them?
What cause did I interject the presence of the Lord on today?

Prayer Emphasis: For the Holy Ghost to reveal specific strategies in proclaiming the Gospel to this community. (Acts 8:26)

Day 26

He has told you, O man, what is good; and what does the LORD require of you but to do justice, and to love kindness, and to walk humbly with your God? Micah 6:8

Morning

Amos 6:12 Do horses run on rocks? Does one plow there with oxen? But you have turned justice into poison and the fruit of righteousness into wormwood—

Ezekiel 25:1 The word of the Lord came to me: "Son of man, set your face toward the Ammonites and prophesy against them. Say to the Ammonites, Hear the word of the Lord God:

Ezekiel 18:21 But if a wicked person turns away from all his sins that he has committed and keeps all my statutes and does what is just and right, he shall surely live; he shall not die.

Ask God to show you a social justice issue in your community to do something about today.

1)
2)
3)

Evening

Yet you have made him a little lower than the heavenly beings and crowned him with glory and honor. Psalm 8:5

Who did I help on today?
How did I help them?
What cause did I interject the presence of the Lord on today?

Prayer Emphasis: That the Holy Ghost will reveal His timing for implementing the strategies of proclamation. (Acts 13:2)

Day 27

He has told you, O man, what is good; and what does the LORD require of you but to do justice, and to love kindness, and to walk humbly with your God? Micah 6:8

Morning

Jeremiah 9:24 But let him who boasts boast in this, that he understands and knows me, that I am the Lord who practices steadfast love, justice, and righteousness in the earth. For in these things I delight, declares the Lord."

Ecclesiastes 3:8 A time to love, and a time to hate; a time for war, and a time for peace.

Psalm 86:13 For great is your steadfast love toward me; you have delivered my soul from the depths of Sheol.

Ask God to show you a social justice issue in your community to do something about today.

1)
2)
3)

Evening

The heavens are the LORD's heavens, but the earth he has given to the children of man. Psalm 115:16

Who did I help on today?
How did I help them?
What cause did I interject the presence of the Lord on today?

Prayer Emphasis: That the Holy Ghost will exalt His name among those who are praying for the gun violence in the community. (Acts 4:31)

____
____
____
____
____
____
____
____

Day 28

He has told you, O man, what is good; and what does the LORD require of you but to do justice, and to love kindness, and to walk humbly with your God? Micah 6:8

Morning

Psalm 67:4 Let the nations be glad in sing for joy, for you judge the peoples with equity and guide the nations upon earth. Selah

Psalm 34:17-18 When the righteous cry for help, the LORD hears and delivers them out of all their troubles. The LORD is near to the brokenhearted and saves the crushed in spirit.

Job 34:12 Of a truth, God will not do wickedly, and the almighty will not pervert justice.

Ask God to show you a social justice issue in your community to do something about today.

1)
2)
3)

Evening

Then a wind from the LORD sprang up, and it brought quail from the sea and let them fall beside the camp, about a day's journey on this side and a day's journey on the other side, around the camp, and about two cubits above the ground. Numbers 11:31

Who did I help on today?
How did I help them?
What cause did I interject the presence of the Lord on today?

Prayer Emphasis: That the Holy Ghost will grant a spirit of persistence in those who are praying for this gun violence community. (Luke 21:36)

Day 29

He has told you, O man, what is good; and what does the LORD require of you but to do justice, and to love kindness, and to walk humbly with your God? Micah 6:8

Morning

2 Chronicles 19:7 Now then, let the fear of the LORD be upon you. Be careful what you do, for there is no injustice with the LORD our God, or partiality or taking bribes."

Deuteronomy 24:17 You shall not pervert the justice due to the sojourner or to the fatherless, or take a widow's garment in pledge,

Exodus 23:6 You shall not pervert the justice due to your poor in his lawsuit.

Ask God to show you a social justice issue in your community to do something about today.

1)
2)
3)

Evening

But love your enemies, and do good, and lend, expecting nothing in return, and your reward will be great, and you will be sons of the Most High, for he is kind to the ungrateful and the evil. Luke 6:35

Who did I help on today?
How did I help them?
What cause did I interject the presence of the Lord on today?

Prayer Emphasis: That the Holy Ghost will proclaim with great clarity and power in this community. (Ephesians 6:17-19)

____
____
____
____
____
____
____
____

Day 30

He has told you, O man, what is good; and what does the LORD require of you but to do justice, and to love kindness, and to walk humbly with your God? Micah 6:8

Morning

Genesis 18:19 For I have chosen him, that he may command his children and his household after him to keep the way of the LORD by doing righteousness and justice, so that the LORD may bring to Abraham what he has promised him."

Psalm 37:27-29 Turn away from evil and do good; so shall you dwell forever. For the LORD loves justice; he will not forsake his saints. They are preserved forever, but the children of the wicked shall be cut off. The righteous shall inherit the land and dwell upon it forever.

Isaiah 55:11 So shall my word be that goes out from my

mouth; it shall not return to me empty, but it shall accomplish that which I purpose, and shall succeed in the thing for which I sent it.

Ask God to show you a social justice issue in your community to do something about today.

1)
2)
3)

Evening

He said, "In a certain city there was a judge who neither feared God nor respected man. And there was a widow in that city who kept coming to him and saying, 'Give me justice against my adversary.' For a while he refused, but afterward he said to himself, 'Though I neither fear God nor respect man, yet because this widow keeps bothering me, I will give her justice, so that she will not beat me down by her continual coming.'" Luke 18:2-5

Who did I help on today?
How did I help them?
What cause did I interject the presence of the Lord on today?

Prayer Emphasis: That the Holy Ghost will create a network of care and support to the families who have suffered from gun violence, and the gospel will be proclaimed. (Philippians 1:18-19)

Notes

Notes

Notes

Additional Readings for Special Occasions

THANKSGIVING

Then they cried to the LORD in their trouble, and he delivered them from their distress. He sent out his word and healed them, and delivered them from their destruction. Let them thank the LORD for his steadfast love, for his wondrous works to the children of man! Psalms 107:19-21

Then Jesus answered, "Were not ten cleansed? Where are the nine? Was no one found to return and give praise to God except this foreigner?" And he said to him, "Rise and go your way; your faith has made you well." Luke 17:17

FOR A BIRTHDAY

The LORD bless you and keep you; the LORD make his face to shine upon you and be gracious to you; the LORD lift up his countenance upon you and give you peace. Numbers 6:24-26

Every place that the sole of your foot will tread upon I have given to you, just as I promised to Moses. Joshua 1:3

FOR TIME OF ANXIETY

O our God, will you not execute judgment on them? For we are powerless against this great horde that is coming against us. We do not know what to do, but our eyes are on you." II Chronicles 20:12

For I, the LORD your God, hold your right hand; it is I who say to you, "Fear not, I am the one who helps you." Isaiah 41:13

MARRIAGE

Let marriage be held in honor among all, and let the marriage bed be undefiled, for God will judge the sexually immoral and adulterous. Keep your life free from love of money, and be content with what you have, for he has said, "I will never leave you nor forsake you." Hebrews 13:4-5

Husbands, love your wives, as Christ loved the church and gave himself up for her, Ephesians 5:25

MARRIAGE THE NEW HOME

I will behave myself wisely in a perfect way. O when wilt thou come unto me? I will walk within my house with a perfect heart. Psalm 101:2

But seek first his kingdom and his righteousness, and all these things will be given to you as well. Matthew 6:33

AFFLICTION

Save me, O God! For the waters have come up to my neck. Psalm 69:1

The steadfast love of the LORD never ceases; his mercies never come to an end; Lamentations 3:22

FOR SICKNESS

So the sisters sent to him, saying, "Lord, he whom you love is ill." But when Jesus heard it he said, "This illness does not lead to death. It is for the glory of God, so that the Son of God may be glorified through it." John 11:3-4

The eternal God is your dwelling place, and underneath are the everlasting arms. And he thrust out the enemy before you and said, 'Destroy.' Deuteronomy 33:27

BEREAVEMENT

Father, I desire that they also, whom you have given me, may be with me where I am, to see my glory that you have given me because you loved me before the foundation of the world. John 17:24

After saying these things, he said to them, "Our friend Lazarus has fallen asleep, but I go to awaken him." John 11:11

UNWELCOME NEWS

But he said to her, "You speak as one of the foolish women would speak. Shall we receive good from God, and shall we not receive evil?" In all this Job did not sin with his lips. Job 2:10

Teach me what I do not see; if I have done iniquity, I will do it no more'? Job 34:32

SEPARATION

"I will not leave you as orphans; I will come to you. John 14:18

Like cold water to a thirsty soul, so is good news from a far country. Proverbs 25:25

RECOVERY FROM SICKNESS

"If you will diligently listen to the voice of the LORD your God, and do that which is right in his eyes, and give ear to his commandments and keep all his statutes, I will put none of the diseases on you that I put on the Egyptians, for I am the LORD, your healer." Exodus 15:26

And the prayer of faith will save the one who is sick, and the Lord will raise him up. And if he has committed sins, he will be forgiven. James 5:15

CONVALESCENCE

Be still before the LORD and wait patiently for him; fret not yourself over the one who prospers in his way, over the man who carries out evil devices! Psalm 37:7

The LORD is your keeper; the LORD is your shade on your right hand. Psalm 121:5

DISAPPOINTED HOPES

In the day of prosperity be joyful, and in the day of adversity consider: God has made the one as well as the other, so that man may not find out anything that will be after him. Ecclesiastes 7:14

Not only that, but we rejoice in our sufferings, knowing that suffering produces endurance, Romans 5:3

DAYS OF PROSPERITY

Let those who delight in my righteousness shout for joy and be glad and say evermore, "Great is the LORD, who delights in the welfare of his servant!" Psalm 35:27

Beloved, I pray that all may go well with you and that you may be in good health, as it goes well with your soul. III John 1:2

SUCCESS

You shall remember the LORD your God, for it is he who gives you power to get wealth, that he may confirm his covenant that he swore to your fathers, as it is this day. Deuteronomy 8:18

Put no trust in extortion; set no vain hopes on robbery; if riches increase, set not your heart on them. Psalm 62:10

THE BIRTH OF A CHILD

For this child I prayed, and the LORD has granted me my petition that I made to him. I Samuel 1:27

A JUBILEE

And you shall consecrate the fiftieth year, and proclaim liberty throughout the land to all its inhabitants. It shall be a jubilee for you, when each of you shall return to his property and each of you shall return to his clan. Leviticus 25:10

For freedom Christ has set us free; stand firm therefore, and do not submit again to a yoke of slavery. Galatians 5:1

LONG LIFE

Wisdom is with the aged, and understanding in length of days. Job 12:12

THE END OF THE JOURNEY

You guide me with your counsel, and afterward you will receive me to glory. Psalm 73:24

Beloved, we are God's children now, and what we will be has not yet appeared; but we know that when he appears we shall be like him, because we shall see him as he is. I John 3:2

Made in the USA
Middletown, DE
14 June 2022